Rock it!

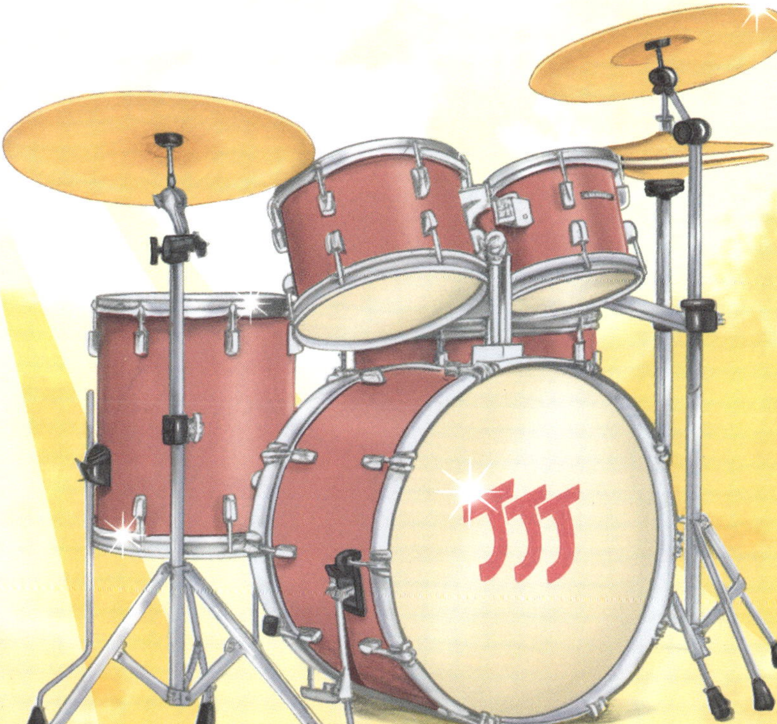

Written by Samantha Montgomerie
Illustrated by Alessandra Sartoris

raintree
a Capstone company — publishers for children

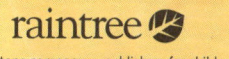

Chapter 1

Da-dum, da-dum, ting!
Jess bashes and bangs on her kit.
The thuds ring out into the night air.

Jess chucks up the sticks. She gets them! Dad winks at Jess.

In the morning, Jess's dad sees an ad. "Rock it at the fair! Rock with us and join in the fun."

Rock it at the fair! Jess thinks that will be a lot of fun.
She gets up, and chucks on her coat and bag. She cannot wait to tell Jin and Jet.

Chapter 2

As soon as she sits down on the bus, Jess gets out the ad for Jin and Jet to look at.

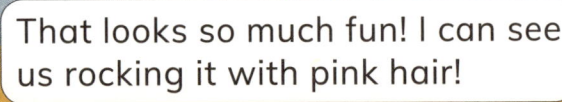

That looks so much fun! I can see us rocking it with pink hair!

Jess looks at the singer, singing under the lights. Jess thinks she looks cool. But Jin looks upset. She will not look at Jess and Jet.

Check it out! We can get set up for the fair in a week. This can be us!

Jin thinks the fair will not be fun for her. Jess pats her on the arm. Jin is such a good singer and she thinks up good songs, too. Jess thinks the kids at the fair will go mad for Jin's singing.

That night, Jess sits on her bed and sighs. She thinks hard. How can she get Jin to sing at the fair?
Think Jess, think! Yes! Jess picks up her tablet. She taps and taps.

To Jin
At the fair, you can sing a song on fear and how to let it go. Tell them all how fear will not keep you back. It will be a big hit!

The tablet dings. Jess looks at it. Yes, Jin is in! She will sing! They are all set to rock!

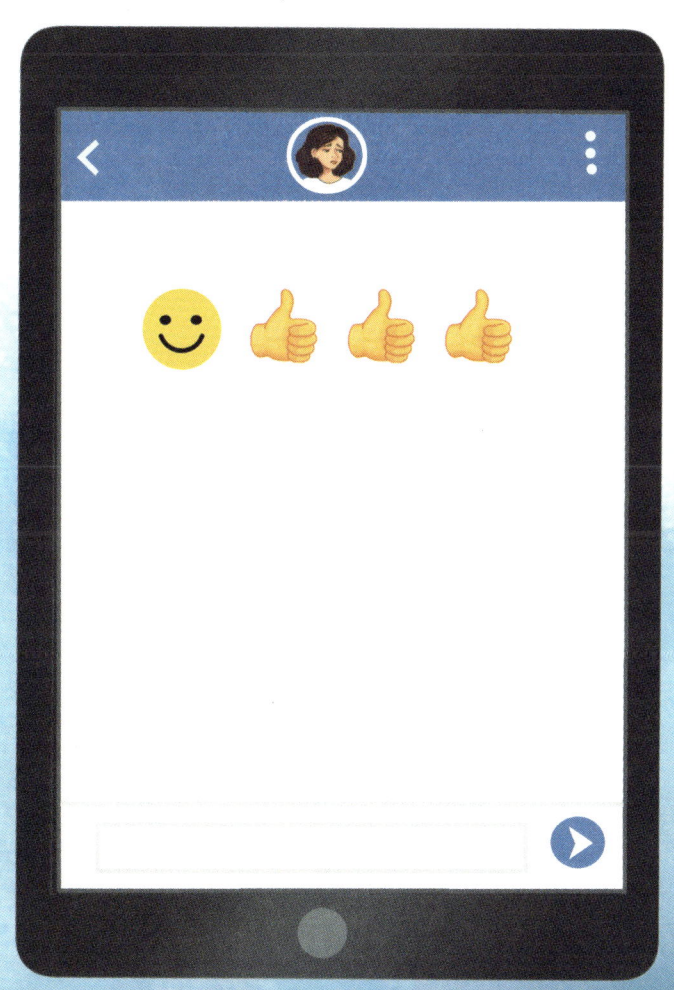

Chapter 3

Jess taps her kit to set them up.
Dum-dum-dum.
Jet joins in. He is good!
Jess bangs and thuds.
Da-dum, da-dum.

Jin gets set to sing. Her fingers tap her leg. Then, she joins in, too.

The rock song fills the air. It is so good.

Let's get this song going!

But will Jin be up to singing at the fair in one week or will it be too soon for her?

Jess, Jin and Jet do the song in Jess's room.
They do the song in Jet's room.
They do the song in Jin's room.
Jess gets good at chucking up her sticks and getting them mid-song.
Jet gets quick at picking his riffs.
Jin lets go and sings her song with all her might.
They **are** going to rock it!

Chapter 4

It's the night of the fair. Jet has pink hair. He is the King of Rock! Jess bows to him.

Jess, Jin and Jet peek out as they wait. The lights are on. They can hear the kids chatting. Then, Jess sees that Jin looks upset. She hugs her.
"You can do this, Jin. Think of the song. Let your fear go! Have fun with it," Jess tells her.

They get set up. The lights are on them, now. Jess chucks up her rods. The room buzzes as she gets them. Jess taps her kit. Jet joins in. But Jess sees Jin look down. "Oh no, Jin cannot sing! Her fear is back," Jess thinks.

Then, Jess sings the song.
She sings as well as she can.

Jet looks back at Jess. He will do this for Jin, too. He sings along with Jess. Jin looks up. The kids are yelling out. Jin will not let her fear in! It will not keep her back! And Jin joins in the singing.

The song fills the air. The room is buzzing. The kids yell as Jin, Jet and Jess sing.

They finish the song.
Jet bows in the lights.
Jess runs up to Jin and hugs her hard.